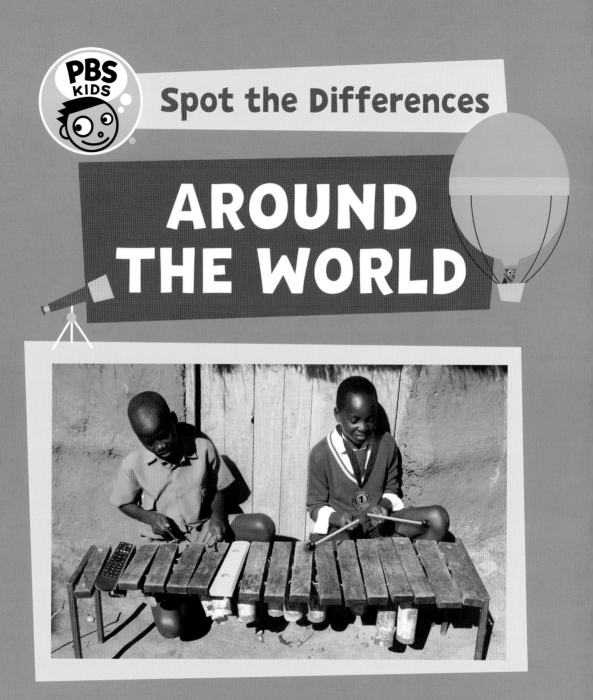

Spot the Differences

AROUND THE WORLD

By Sarah Parvis and Georgia Rucker

downtown 🏙 bookworks

Downtown Bookworks Inc.
265 Canal Street, New York, NY 10013

Copyright © 2019 by Downtown Bookworks Inc.
By Sarah Parvis
Designed by Georgia Rucker
Printed in China, June 2019

10 9 8 7 6 5 4 3 2 1

PHOTO CREDITS Front cover: ©iStock.com/coramueller (bear), photopixel/Shutterstock.com (flags), Africa Studio/Shutterstock.com (balloons), FeellFree/Shutterstock.com (sunglasses), ©iStock.com/RASimon (beach ball). Interior: 1: CECIL BO DZWOWA/Shutterstock.com (boys), BaLL LunLa/Shutterstock.com (remote), olegganko/Shutterstock.com (yellow bar), Roman Samborskyi/Shutterstock.com (medal), Alexei Zatevakhin/Shutterstock.com (mallets). 3: Natalia Barsukova/Shutterstock.com (flamingos), Oleksii Lomako/Shutterstock.com (float), Africa Studio/Shutterstock.com (necklace). 4: Song_about_summer/Shutterstock.com (Antarctica), untitled/Shutterstock.com (float), oobqoo/Shutterstock.com (ripped jeans), ©iStock.com/RyanJLane (fanny pack). 5: Dietmar Temps/Shutterstock.com (Madagascar), WilleeCole Photography/Shutterstock.com (glasses), ChiccoDodiFC/Shutterstock.com (weather vane). 6: Alexey Fedorenko/Shutterstock.com (Scotland, flag), Weho/Shutterstock.com (bear), New Africa/Shutterstock.com (fingers). 7: Benny Marty/Shutterstock.com (Greece), Jakkrit Orrasri/Shutterstock.com (bone), otsphoto/Shutterstock.com (leash), Dimitrios/Shutterstock.com (statue). 8: ©iStock.com/swissmediavision (New Zealand, new legs), Cherdchai charasri/Shutterstock.com (basketball), Doug Lemke/Shutterstock.com (lighthouse), Alex Bard/Shutterstock.com (tail). 9: muratart/Shutterstock.com (Turkey), Lizard/Shutterstock.com (flag), Elena Rostunova/Shuttertstock.com (turret), Thye-Wee Gn/Shutterstock.com (chairs), Mrs_ya/Shutterstock.com (red carpet). 10: Ko Backpacko/Shutterstock.com (Myanmar), vander/Shutterstock.com (clock), donatas1205/Shutterstock.com (buttons), Roman Samokhin/Shutterstock.com (watermelon), asharkyu/Shutterstock.com (ivy). 11: Natalia Kirichenko/Shutterstock.com (Australia), Valentina Razumova/Shutterstock.com (carrot). 12: CroMary/Shutterstock.com (Netherlands), Anna Maloverjan/Shutterstock.com (ponytail), Butterfly Hunter/Shutterstock.com (butterfly), Hekla/Shutterstock.com (hand), Dmitry Zimin/Shutterstock.com (umbrella). 13: Deborah Augsburger/Shutterstock.com (Bolivia), stifos/Shutterstock.com (llama sign), Byelikova Oksana/Shutterstock.com (cactus), Krasowit/Shutterstock.com (fish), Africa Studio/Shutterstock.com (scarf). 14: Marvin Minder/Shutterstock.com (Costa Rica, new sloth), StudioSmart/Shutterstock.com (bear), Evdokimov Maxim/Shutterstock.com (bow). 15: Arsenie Krasnevsky/Shutterstock.com (France), photomaster/Shutterstock.com (falcon), OrangeGroup/Shutterstock.com (pant leg), railway fx/Shutterstock.com (flag). 16: Vixit/Shutterstock.com (Maldives, flip-flops), Baanrukbua/Shutterstock.com (coconuts), RUTiAM/Shutterstock.com (bear). 17: MikeDotta/Shutterstock.com (Egypt), topseller/Shutterstock.com (hot-air balloon). 18: BlueOrange Studio/Shutterstock.com (Norway), Piotr Piatrouski/Shutterstock.com (igloo), Dzha33/Shutterstock.com (horn), Irina Rogova/Shutterstock.com (tree). 19: Sun_Shine/Shutterstock.com (Tanzania), S_Photo/Shutterstock.com (sand art), Vereshchagin Dmitry/Shutterstock.com (sail), Kues/Shutterstock.com (scales), Ruth Black/Shutterstock.com (lollipop). 20: MinhHue/Shutterstock.com (all). 21: SvetlanaSF/Shutterstock.com (Bahamas), Calvste/Shutterstock.com (feathers), Eric Isselee/Shutterstock.com (chipmunk). 22: Olexandr Taranukhin/Shutterstock.com (Ukraine), ekapol sirachainan/Shutterstock.com (keyboard), goir/Shutterstock.com (sign), Mark_KA/Shutterstock.com (cat), Iasha/Shutterstock.com (bat). 23: lunamarina/Shutterstock.com (Mexico), Nuttapong/Shutterstock.com (hat), Dmitry Rukhlenko/Shutterstock.com (blue statue). 24: Chrispictures/Shutterstock.com (Colombia), Amam ka/Shutterstock.com (soccer balls). 25: ©iStock.com/filipefrazao (Brazil), pukach/Shutterstock.com (balloon), Ruslan Kudrin/Shutterstock.com (flower). 26: Wutthichai/Shutterstock.com (Thailand), april70/Shutterstock.com (new flower), Ekkoss/Shutterstock.com (cactus), saravutpics/Shutterstock.com (pillar). 27: Anna Jedynak/Shutterstock.com (Cuba), Cameris/Shutterstock.com (signal), Sabino Parente/Shutterstock.com (flag). 28: PawelG Photo/Shutterstock.com (Germany), George3973/Shutterstock.com (hard pretzel), rayjunk/Shutterstock.com (mustard). 29: Grigvovan/Shutterstock.com (Iran), Veniamin Kraskov/Shutterstock.com (watering can, pinwheel), canbedone/Shutterstock.com (doll), design56/Shutterstock.com (backpack). 30–31: Max Topchii/Shutterstock.com. 31: Suzanne Tucker/Shutterstock.com (eyeballs), muratart/Shutterstock.com (dolphins), visionaryft/Shutterstock.com (flippers). 32: Hung Chung Chih/Shutterstock.com (China), Diego Gutierrez Yrizar/Shutterstock.com (streetlight), LUMPANG MOONMUANG/Shutterstock.com (glove), Mega Pixel/Shutterstock.com (peace sign), VAV/Shutterstock.com (chalk). 33: SL-Photography/Shutterstock.com (Peru, new head), Serge Siro/Shutterstock.com (wall). 34: norikko/Shutterstock.com (Japan, soy sauce), Africa Studio/Shutterstock.com (chopsticks). 35: CECIL BO DZWOWA/Shutterstock.com (Zimbabwe), BaLL LunLa/Shutterstock.com (remote), olegganko/Shutterstock.com (yellow bar), Roman Samborskyi/Shutterstock.com (medal), Alexei Zatevakhin/Shutterstock.com (mallets). 36–37: Gilmanshin/Shutterstock.com. 37: Ruth Black/Shutterstock.com (cupcake), Dan Kosmayer/Shutterstock.com (chocolate), yukihipo/Shutterstock.com (birthday hat), defpicture/Shutterstock.com (window). 38: MarkLG/Shutterstock.com (all). 39: Quick Shot/Shutterstock.com (Mali), Richard Peterson/Shutterstock.com (ladder), Ljupco Smokovski/Shutterstock.com (seesaw), Heike Brauer/Shutterstock.com (cone). 40–41: SAPhotog/Shutterstock.com. 41: New Vibe/Shutterstock.com (flower), Taweesak Sriwannawit/Shutterstock.com (lantern). 42: Drop of Light/Shutterstock.com (Vatican City), terekhov igor/Shutterstock.com (broom), Anton Starikov/Shutterstock.com (pom-pom), Benjamin Miner/Shutterstock.com (toy soldier), TaraPatta/Shutterstock.com (door). 43: Amy Nichole Harris/Shutterstock.com (Chile), Anthony Booker/Shutterstock.com (new statue), Alberto Loyo/Shutterstock.com (boulder), SUPAPORNKH/Shutterstock.com (flowers), OSORIOartist/Shutterstock.com (horse). 44–45: Angela N Perryman/Shutterstock.com. 45: Chanita Chokchaikul/Shutterstock.com (bangs), Kate Pi/Shutterstock.com (flower). 46: Cynthia Liang/Shutterstock.com (England), Dan Kosmayer/Shutterstock.com (ice cream), Sanit Fuangnakhon/Shutterstock.com (tree). 47: ©iStock.com/hadynyah (India), vetre/Shutterstock.com (sandcastle), LifetimeStock/Shutterstock.com (fennec fox). 48–49: ziggy_mars/Shutterstock.com. 49: fewerton/Shutterstock.com (sunglasses), Akitameldes/Shutterstock.com (dog). 50: GuoZhongHua/Shutterstock.com (Cambodia), iFocus/Shutterstock.com (stuffed elephant), Chimpinski/Shutterstock.com (top hat), nasidastudio/Shutterstock.com (trunk), bergamont/Shutterstock.com (bananas). 51: chythaiphotocyber/Shutterstock.com (Switzerland), ragophotos/Shutterstock.com (cow), LightField Studios/Shutterstock.com (tool belt), elena_timiy/Shutterstock.com (goo), Aleksandar Grozdanovski/Shutterstock.com (valves), Photo Melon/Shutterstock.com (kite). 52: Aleksei Potov/Shutterstock.com (Canada), Checubus/Shutterstock.com (bear sign), Susan Schmitz/Shutterstock.com (dog), thechatat/Shutterstock.com (alligator), Iasha/Shutterstock.com (hockey stick), Smit/Shutterstock.com (tree). 53: David Steele/Shutterstock.com (UAE), Pixeljoy/Shutterstock.com (pirate flag), Lilu330/Shutterstock.com (sticker), Erin Donalson/Shutterstock.com (whale tail). 54: Anton_Ivanov/Shutterstock.com (Ghana), mmalkani/Shutterstock.com (flower print), Punchalit Chotiksatian/Shutterstock.com (lei), Karkas/Shutterstock.com (purse). 55: Nokuro/Shutterstock.com (Malaysia), Gavran333/Shutterstock.com (new tongs), Bryan Solomon/Shutterstock.com (chocolate donut). 56: StockphotoVideo/Shutterstock.com (Latvia), Shvaygert Ekaterina/Shutterstoc.com (gum), Ukki Studio/Shutterstock.com (heart), Wuttichok Panichiwarapun/Shutterstock.com (ukulele), Nenad Nedomacki/Shutterstock.com (face paint). 57: FuGazi images/Shutterstock.com (Morocco), Andrei Kholmov/Shutterstock.com (pizza), LongQuattro/Shutterstock.com (tire tracks), Peter Turner Photography/Shutterstock.com (flower pot), MirasWonderland/Shutterstock.com (cat). Back cover: CroMary/Shutterstock.com (Netherlands), Anna Maloverjan/Shutterstock.com (ponytail), Butterfly Hunter/Shutterstock.com (butterfly), Hekla/Shutterstock.com (hand), Dmitry Zimin/Shutterstock.com (umbrella).

Spot the Differences

Look at each pair of pictures. Point at everything that is different. And count the differences you find.

Hi, parents! As your kids do these puzzles, tell them to look out for:

- **items that have appeared or disappeared**
- **things that have gotten larger or smaller or shorter or longer**
- **colors that have changed**
- **objects that have been replaced with something new**

If your child is stumped, remind them to look closely at each picture and how they are different.

**You can even ask questions to help.
Are all of the trees the same?
Do all of the flamingoes' necks look the same?
Is there anything new in the water?**

This number tells you how many differences are in the puzzle.

The puzzles get more challenging as you go!

Fabulous Flamingos   Point to **4** differences   Aruba

Spot the differences puzzles are a great workout for visual observation and spatial relations skills. Encourage your child to celebrate each find by saying what they spotted aloud. Naming objects, colors, and size differences will also boost your child's vocabulary and confidence—plus, it's fun!

Antarctica

Beautiful Boat by the Sea

Madagascar

Scotland

Rover Among the Ruins

Point to **4** differences

Greece

Boulders on the Beach

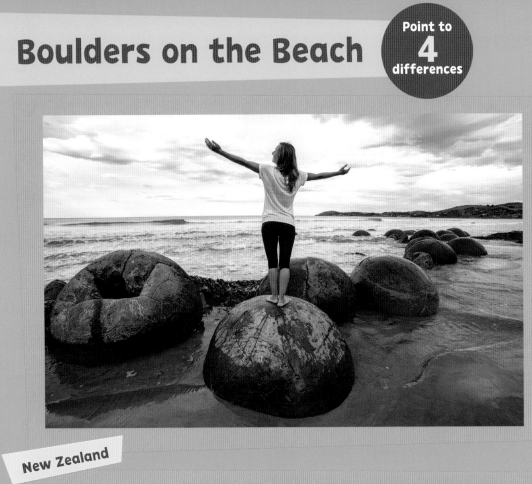

New Zealand

Welcome to Topkapi Palace

Turkey

Monks Play Ball Too!

Point to
4
differences

Myanmar

10

Hoppy Kangaroos

Point to **4** differences

Australia

11

Delightful Dutch Day

The Netherlands

Llama Drama

Point to **4** differences

Bolivia

Baby Sloth

Point to 4 differences

Costa Rica

France

Island Time

The Maldives

Camel Kisses

Point to

4

differences

Egypt

Point to
4
differences

Norway

Sun, Sand, and Scales

Tanzania

Let's Play Catch!

Vietnam

Point to
4
differences

The Bahamas

Ukraine

Iguana's Day Out

Point to **4** differences

Mexico

23

Colombia

Brazil

Thailand

Taxi! Taxi!

Cuba

Pretzel Perfection

Point to **5** differences

Germany

School Friends

Iran

Walking on the Great Wall

China

Relaxing in a Row

Point to
5
differences

Peru

33

Xylophone Practice

Point to **5** differences

Zimbabwe

St. Basil's Birthday Bash!

Italy

An Amazing Mosque

Mali

Don't Forget Your Lunch

Vatican City

Chile

Ice Cream for the Queen!

England

Desert Stroll

India

Ready for School

An Elephant Ride

Point to **6** differences

Cambodia

Alphorns in the Alps

Switzerland

Canada

Sailboat Race

Point to **6** differences

United Arab Emirates

Ghana

Snack Time!

Malaysia

Latvia

Watch Out!

Morocco

57

Answer Key

front cover

p. 3

p. 4

p. 5

p. 6

p. 7

p. 8

p. 9

p. 13

p. 10

p. 14

p. 11

p. 15

p. 12

p. 16

Answer Key

p. 17

p. 18

p. 19

p. 20

p. 21

p. 22

p. 23

p. 24

p. 25

p. 29

p. 26

p. 30–31

p. 27

p. 32

p. 28

p. 33

Answer Key

p. 34

p. 35

p. 36–37

p. 38

p. 39

p. 40–41

p. 42

p. 43

p. 48–49

p. 44–45

p. 50

p. 46

p. 51

p. 47

p. 52

p. 53

p. 56

p. 54

p. 57

p. 55

Special thanks to all our puzzle testers and their helpers: Joanna Schlesser-Perry, Kai Schlesser, and Aiden Williams; Christina and Vincent Vermillion; Selina Greene and Oliver Cooper; Bryan Giansanti and Hollis and Harper Giansanti Stokes; Lana, Carter, and Mona O'Brien; Josiah and Davis Trager; Sarah, Jameson, and Annabelle Tormey; Nana and Archer Skye Lamouse-Welch; and Ari Barbanell Kassirer and Ellington Kassirer.